"Lessons Learned After Dark"

Conquering Cancer and other Life Challenges

By: *Gaylon P. Foreman*

No matter how much you love God or how long you've been truly walking with Him, there are some lessons that can not truly be learned until you're in a dark place in your life

Gaylon P. Foreman

Lessons Learned After Dark

Lessons Learned After Dark

Dedications

To my late parents, William and Undree Foreman, who spent their entire lives preparing me and my nine brothers and sisters to live positive and productive lives.

To my wife of 28 years, D. Yvette, who gives significance and meaning to my life. The love and support you give helps me to stay positive and productive even in tough and trying times. I love you more today than yesterday and even more tomorrow!!!

To my children, Shelby Janay and Gaylon Jermon, who make my life a joy even when I'm going through sad or sorrowful times. I love you to life!!!

To Sis. Sophia A. Strother and Pastor David Burrus for your help and encouragement throughout this entire project. You'll never know how much it means to me to have awesome people like you in my life.

Last, but not least, to my *Lord and Savoir Jesus Christ* for ordering my steps and allowing the right people to cross my path at the appointed time. I'm eternally grateful for you allowing me to be a part of what you're doing in this season!!!

Lessons Learned After Dark

Lessons Learned After Dark

Printed in the United States of America

All scripture references are from the King James Version of the Holy Bible.

ISBN-13: 978-1482005301

ISBN-10: 1482005301

No part of this book may be used or reproduced without the written permission of the publisher. Publisher and Writer information:

> Gaylon Foreman
> 1020 E. Herring Ave
> Waco, Texas 76704
> gp4man@aol.com
> (254) 799-2766

Copyright @ 2013 Gaylon P. Foreman

Front Cover Design by: Pastor David Burris

Back Cover Design by: Gaylon P. Foreman

Cover and interior Photo by: Marcus Johnson

Edited by: Sophia A. Strother

This book is an honest and accurate account of a period in my life when I was diagnosed, treated, and healed from cancer. All noted incidents are part of my life's experience and reflect some of the valuable lessons that the Lord has used in my life to teach me.

First Edition.

Lessons Learned After Dark

Lessons Learned After Dark

About the Author

Gaylon Paul Foreman is a native of Fort Worth, Texas. He is the fifth of ten children born to William and Undree Foreman. In 1980, he felt led of God to move to Waco, Texas to attend Paul Quinn College. While attending PQC, he met and married the former Doris Yvette Carey. They are blessed to have two wonderful children, Shelby and Jermon.

Gaylon is the Senior Pastor of Carver Park Baptist Church, where he has faithfully served since 1990. He holds a Bachelor in Social Work, Master of Education in Counseling and a Doctorate in Clinical Pastoral Counseling.

This book is a reflection of a time in his life when he truly learned to trust in the Lord at a deeper level.

Be blessed as you learn lessons after dark!!!

Lessons Learned After Dark

Lessons Learned After Dark

Table of Contents

Preschool

Lesson 1: You can't control what comes your way, but you can control your response

Lesson 2: Be careful who you listen to

Lesson 3: You must know that God can heal instantly, but doesn't always do so

Lesson 4: Preaching through a storm

Lesson 5: What you go through is often not about you

Conclusion of the Matter

Lessons Learned After Dark

Lessons Learned After Dark

Preschool

Lessons Learned After Dark

Lessons Learned After Dark

Preschool

The year was 2010 and it was looking like the greatest year of my life. The year started with Latter Glory, our week of worship, where we start the year off right by giving God the firstfruit of our year. The following weekend, my wife and I renewed our wedding vows to celebrate 25 year of marriage. My daughter was scheduled to graduate at the end of the year and my son was about to sign a basketball scholarship with an area Junior College. As if that wasn't enough, I was serving as Pastor of the greatest church this side of heaven and they were planning our 20th Pastoral Appreciation. Who could ask for anything more? Life was looking extremely bright and I was living and loving life to the max. However, in the midst of the celebrating the Lord, His goodness, and the life that He had given me, something happened that changed my life forever.

I've often said that no matter how awesome the mountaintop experience is, you can not live on the mountaintop. Just like you rise up and rejoice while life is one celebration after another, you can rest assured that there will be some low places in your life. The issue is what do you do when you find yourself in life's valley? Do you cry, complain and wonder

Lessons Learned After Dark

"Why me?" or do you continue to rejoice and bless the Lord for His goodness? I had preached and taught for years about how a valley is just a dance floor between the mountaintop that you're leaving and the one that you're heading to and how we should keep dancing, even in tough and trying times. I was about to be tested to see if I could really practice what I preached.

Night cometh

My wife and I were preparing for bed and I felt what I thought was an insect bite or sting on the side of my neck. Not thinking much of it, I rubbed some alcohol on the spot and began to relax and wind down from a hectic day. Instead of my neck feeling better, it started to feel worse, so I asked my wife to look at it and see if she could tell if a stinger or something may have been still beneath the skin. When she looked at it, her silence let me know that there was something wrong. I asked her what was wrong and she replied I don't think it's a bite or sting unless you're allergic to whatever bit or stung you. She explained to me that my neck was extremely swollen and that I might need to go to the emergency room. We prayed and I convinced her that we could set an appointment with our Family Physician in the morning and find out what was wrong.

Lessons Learned After Dark

We went to sleep as usual and still anticipated waking to an awesome day.

The Clinic opened at 8:00am and at 7:59am, my wife called the clinic to see if our Family Physician would be able to fit me in and of course, we were able to be seen that morning. Our Physician looked at my neck, asked a lot of questions about and prescribed some antibiotics to treat the possible insect bite or sting. He also made it clear that if it was not better in a week that he wanted to see me again. A week past and nothing changed, so we returned to our Physician and he suggested a Specialist take a look at it and he scheduled the appointment. The Specialist looked at my neck, asked a lot of questions, and then suggested a biopsy. He scheduled the biopsy for the end of the week and the procedure went well, but we had to wait until the following week to get the results.

The First Major Quiz

On March 15th, we went in for the results. We sat down and waited for the Specialist to come in and I must admit that 15 minutes seemed like hours. The door opened, he shook my hand, sat down and with no expression of kindness or bed side manner simply said "Mr. Foreman, I hate to tell you, but you have cancer". He paused for a few seconds and said, "I'll schedule an appointment for you at Texas Oncology to see if they can develop some type of treatment plan or see what they can do…I wish you well". He then asked if we had any questions or anything that we wanted to discuss with him. I said "No nothing that I could think of" and as strange as it seemed, I told him "Thank you" and stood to shake his hand. He headed out, but said that we could sit there for a few minutes, if we needed a little time alone.

After about a minute or so, my wife said she needed to use the restroom and would meet me at the car. Of course, after being married to her for 25 years, I knew that she was in shock and needed a good cry and a chance to pray that feeling away. I walked toward the exit and waited for about 5 minutes or so and she came out, with her brave face on. It was obvious to me that she had been crying and was still hurting, so I reassured her that I was fine and that healing and wholeness was already mine. We hugged, a few tears fell and we both thanked God for healing and wholeness before getting in the car and heading home. As we drove, we prayed about how to tell our children and the rest of the family.

Lessons Learned After Dark

We got home and our daughter was there and asked what we had found out. I tried to be gentle as I told her that they had found some cancerous cells in my neck and that we were going to meet with a Specialist in a couple of days regarding treatment. At the mention of the word cancerous, tears began to flow and we held her tightly and reassured her that my healing was already done. My son was in Temple in school and had called about needing groceries, so we used that as a reason to come to see him. We picked him up and as we drove to the local grocery store and were getting out the car to walk toward the store, I explained to him about the cancerous cells and the need for treatment. He embraced me and his mom and a few tears fell, but as we told him that healing was already done, he stopped and gathered himself and said that he believed it because we said it. We used the rest of the day to call our family members and reassure them that we were fine and that there was nothing to worry about. Everyone seemed to accept the news well and now it was just a matter of waiting to meet with my Oncologist and see what, if anything he had in mind as far as treatment.

Such was the beginning of the lessons that I had to learn after dark!!!!

Lessons Learned After Dark

Lessons Learned After Dark

Lesson 1

You can't always control what comes your way, but you can control your response.

Lessons Learned After Dark

Lessons Learned After Dark

Lesson 1

You can't always control what comes your way, but you can control your response.

No matter how thought out your plan may be, life has a way of throwing a wrench into those plans. Think about, as a child you had dreams that were without limits and you heard that you could be anything that you wanted to be. Can you honestly say that your dreams have not changed from childhood and that you're living the life that you dreamed and planned for? I'm not saying that there are no men or women who stuck with a dream and plan and have not altered them over the years, but that is not the testimony of most. Life has caused most of us to change and adjust and rethink things, for many it's been multiple times.

Examples to consider

(1) There are many of us who fell in love with athletics, during our youth and had dreams of being the next great player in the NFL, NBA, MLB, WNBA, etc. Some were great high school athletes and kept the dream alive by going on to play college athletics only to find that in college there were many who were as good and some

even better. There were some who were great in college and even got a shot at the pros, only to find out that they were a great college athlete, but not ready for the pros. There were even a few who made it to the pros and enjoyed a great career, only to find out that it ended a lot sooner than they expected. The truth of the matter is that you couldn't control what happened to you, but you could decide how you would respond. For those who were ready to adapt and make the best of their situations, they found some area where they could move forward and succeed. For those who could not adapt, they often ended up frustrated with life and unable to move forward. In many cases, they become that parent that pushes their child to hard and takes the fun out of athletics by trying to live through their child instead of letting the child enjoy being a child.

(2) There are those who fell in love or lust in high school and/or college and dreamed of living happily ever after with the love of your life. Some didn't make it through high school or college before your plans fell apart. Others made it through high school and college and even made it to the altar and married the person of their

dreams. As time went by, they found themselves unhappy or even miserable trying to hold on to that dream and fight through the problems and issues, only to end up divorced and alone. For those who could adapt and regroup, they picked themselves up, dusted themselves off and moved forward. For those who couldn't adapt, they spend years either longing for what use to be or trying to discover another Mr. or Mrs. Right, while using the criteria from your first relationship. Failing to realize that you can't safely and successfully move forward while looking backward!

(3) There are those who found a job or career that they loved and dreamed of working there until they reached retirement. The great salary, benefits, and company seemed to be tailor made for them and they couldn't see themselves doing anything else. Then one day, the business was not as lucrative as it once was and the company had to downsize. Of course, they're not worried because they're an excellent employee who had proven to perform quality work, so of course they're certainly safe. However, they get that call to meet with the boss and still they don't think they're in danger of

losing their job and/or career. Then they get the word that they've been a faithful employee and asset to the company, but regrettably, they have to let them go. For those who are able to adapt, you gather yourself either finding another company that values skills that you possess or you use this as a chance to venture out into your own business. For those who can't adapt, they become bitter and angry and if they're not careful will lose years of valuable time feeling down and discouraged, while life just passes by. Many fail to realize that sometimes what looks like a closed door is in all actuality an open opportunity to greater things!

Remember that you can't control what comes your way, but you have the final say in how you will respond.

Lessons Learned After Dark

<u>In my case</u>

When the Physician said "I'm sorry but you have cancer" and basically sounded like he didn't think I would make it, I had a choice to make. Either I was going to take my cue from him and begin to feel sorry for myself and begin planning my funeral or I was going to prepare to do whatever I had to do to overcome this diagnosis. No doubt many would have bought in to the Physician's negative vibe and prepared to die, but for me that was never an option. Think about it, I have an awesome wife, two wonderful children, a great family that looks up to me, a blessed bunch of Believers that look to me for leadership and a whole lot of living to do! As I thought about all of that, the Spirit of God reminded me of what the Physician said "you have cancer" and what I heard was I have it, but it doesn't have me, which meant I had the final say. I must be honest, the enemy tried his best to attack my mind and tell me that I wasn't going to make it and that I should begin making funeral arrangements, but the Spirit of God wouldn't let that thought stick. The Lord brought scripture after scripture to my mind about the promises of healing and I begin to speak them over my life as if my life depended on it. Every time the enemy threw a negative thought, I countered it with the word of God. The more I confessed the word over my life and situation, the stronger I felt. I truly learned to confess *"greater is He that is in me than he that is in the world"* and the Greater One kept on showing Himself mighty on my behalf.

It doesn't matter what you're going through or how bad things may look in your life right now, you have to recognize that you have the final say in how you'll respond. You're not at the mercy of your circumstances nor does your situation have any power over you. It may seem like it's impossible, but remember *"with God all things are possible"*. You may feel like you've gone as far as you can go, done all that you can do and feel like all your hope and strength is gone, but remember *"the Lord strength is made perfect in our weakness"*.

When you're down to nothing, God is always up to something and it's up to you to trust and obey Him. You have to be so confident in God that you can still celebrate while you wait. Think about it, anybody can bless the Lord when everything is going well, but true Worshippers can praise through pain, shout in the midst of sorrow, and bless God while burdened.

Life may have hit you with a spiritual gut punch, but now that you've had time to catch your breath, what are you going to

Lessons Learned After Dark

do? I suggest that you learn how to take authority over your situation and continue to say what God says about it in His word. Speak life even if it looks like and you even feel like you're dying. There is power in your words!!!

Declare and decree it until you see it!!!

Lessons Learned After Dark

Lessons Learned After Dark

Lesson 2

Be Careful who you listen to!

Lessons Learned After Dark

Lessons Learned After Dark

Lesson 2
Be Careful who you listen to!

On Sunday March 21st, I asked the church family to stay after our Morning Celebration, so that I could share something with them. In 20 years of serving as Pastor of Carver Park, I had never kept anything from them, so I knew that I had to tell them about my diagnosis. I preached that morning and we had an awesome and anointed celebration. The Spirit of God moved mightily and souls were saved, several rededications, and the altar was filled with those who were seeking the Lord in prayer. I felt so refreshed and renewed, but then came the moment to share the news with my church family. I called my wife and children up to stand with me and I figured that it would be as simple as just saying it, but it wasn't.

I opened up by telling them that in 20 years, I had always been totally open and honest with them and that I wanted to share something important with them. It seemed like a weight just came upon me and the people seemed to be weighted down also. As I began to speak, my voice began to crack and tears started flowing down my cheeks. I didn't cry when I was diagnosed or when I told my children, but as I tried to tell our church family, I was just overwhelmed. Even so, I told them that I had been diagnosed with cancer and at this point had no idea what type of treatment would be recommended or even if they would recommend a treatment. Before I finished my statement, I could see tears flowing throughout the sanctuary, so I quickly reminded them that no matter what, I was going to be fine because *"by His stripes, I am healed"*. That seemed to ease some of the concern and to be honest, when I declared it, I felt stronger also. I asked that they respect me and my family's privacy and allow us to ease out without any questions or anything and I assured them that I would be there Wednesday night ready to minister as usual. We left out the side exit, went home, and tried to rest and relax, but by the time we got home, the phone started ringing off the hook and I really started to learn about the importance of who you listen to.

Examples to consider

(1) There are many of us who have been told what we couldn't do or have been criticized and questioned about our abilities and/qualifications. Like David, whose own father didn't think enough of him to invite him in from the field, when the Prophet came to anoint one of his sons as King; many of us have been

overlooked. We've basically been invisible to many people because they can only see us at the level we were when they met us. They still see you as the little boy, with the hot temper who was always getting in trouble or the little girl who always had something to say and stayed in trouble because you didn't know when to keep quiet. Even though you've grown and you're much more mature and in some cases raising children of your own, they still see your past instead of your present and/or future. It's vitally important that you know that *"you are fearfully and wonderfully made"* and that you not allow anyone to frame your future with negative confessions. Never allow someone else's blurred vision of you cause you to see yourself as less that blessed!

(2) There are many who have made major mistakes and have had to pay the price. Maybe you've served time, been in rehab or been through some things that you regret, but at the end of the day, what you've been through is not who you are. Although there will be those who will always find some way to remind you of your past, your job is to stay focused on your glorious

future. You've got to believe that the rest of your days are the best of your days and that your latter is going to be greater than your past. Even though you can't stop people from saying what they will, you can make sure that you don't receive any of the negative, counterproductive things that they say. *"Death and life are in the power of the tongue"*, so you have to make sure that you maintain a positive outlook and confession and speak life even into those situations that may be in a coma or on life support. Learn not to listen to everyone who has something to say and even that which you have to hear, *"try the Spirit by the Spirit"* to see if it's worthy of even entertaining. Even some who mean well can distract you from your destiny by trying to get you to play it safe when God is trying to stretch you!

Lessons Learned After Dark

<u>In my case</u>

I mentioned earlier that as soon as we got home, our phone started ringing and I already had a countless number of messages. There were calls from the city, throughout the state, and even from around the country. The number of calls was overwhelming as I didn't even realize I knew that many people. There were Pastors, Ministers, and members from every faith, but surprisingly many of them spoke as if they were calling to express their sympathy. I was so shocked at the number of people who were professing faith in Jesus Christ, but talking like all hope was lost. After a few of those sad, sorrowful calls, I just stopped answering the phone and just listened to messages after they had accumulated. There were the calls that would have made me depressed if I didn't have faith in God, but also a caller who prophesied that I didn't have cancer and that the Doctors were wrong and it was a plot of the enemy to silence one of God's mighty men.

When you consider the number of calls and the various messages that were given, I had to truly be careful about who I listened to. The Lord made it clear as far as which ones were actually speaking as His representatives as well as those who didn't have a clue. He connected me with a faithful few, who were committed to His will and to praying for and with me as well as doing all that they could to help me through what I was going through. I must admit that I spoke with very few people on a regular basis because I was already aware of the need to speak over and into my life and the situation that I was dealing with. So daily, I sought the Lord for guidance and strength for the journey and also listened attentively to everything that He said to me. The more that I listened to the Lord and less I listened to people, the stronger I got. I had to not return some calls and not listen to some of the people who crossed my path because even the well intended didn't know what the Lord was saying to me and couldn't say anything that would help my situations.

Death and life are in the power of the tongue and I was speaking life and could not afford to surround myself with people who were speaking death.

One of the greatest lessons that anyone can learn is to watch who you allow to speak into and over your life!!!

Lessons Learned After Dark

Lesson 3

You must know that God can heal instantly, but doesn't always do so!!!

Lessons Learned After Dark

Lessons Learned After Dark

Lesson 3
You must know that God can heal instantly, but doesn't always do so!!!

In my lifetime, I've seen time and time again where God healed and/or deliver people with just a word of prayer. Countless time, He has had me have prayer lines or altar call and lay hands on the sick and see them be recovered. I am convinced and convicted and have absolutely no doubt about the Lord being a Healer and still healing of every kind of disease and/or sickness. However, to be honest it has crossed my mind and even been asked in bible study, what about those cases where the Lord does not heal. Of course my answer has always been that He's still God and has total control of every situation on earth and in heaven. This belief was tested and I thank God that I passed the tests!!!

After being diagnosed with cancer, there was a two week period between the diagnosis and the initial visit with the Oncologist. I was so confident in God that dying only crossed my mind a couple of times and both times, I rebuked the thought and declared my healing and wholeness, in Jesus' name. The test was not whether I would believe God or not, but whether I could handle God not handling my situation as I expected. You see, I knew that healing and wholeness were already mine, but the actual manifestation was a different thing.

I had prayed for the sick even the week before I was diagnosed and had received a Praise Report that one of those that I prayed for. This person had an appointment the same week that I did and the Doctors were amazed and acknowledged that they could no longer see the growth that they were preparing to remove. So things were just right for God to show up and show out on my behalf. I daily laid hands on myself, had Prayer Warriors standing in agreement with me and friends as well as family lifting me in prayer. I was excited about the two week window of opportunity and just knew that when I went in to see the Oncologist that he was going to say that he didn't see the cancerous cells that were seen two weeks earlier. I mean why God wouldn't show Himself mighty and get the Glory out of this situation.

I walked in to the Texas Oncology office, signed in and waited for my name to be called. Still excited about what God was

Lessons Learned After Dark

about to do in this office on this day. They called me to the back, took my vitals and had me to be seated in a treatment room. After about 5-7 minutes, Dr Anderson walked in and introduced himself. I was still excited and waiting for him to give me the good news that they no longer saw the growth. Long story short, he not only saw the growth, but had a treatment plan ready to discuss with me. He told me that he was convinced that he had a plan that would give me the best possible chance for a total recovery. I thanked him and went to the desk to schedule my first session of chemotherapy for the following week.

As I got to my car, I asked the Lord about it. Not questioning God or His sovereignty in any way, but seeking clarity about my situation. Like I said, I'd prayed for so many others and watched them be healed, but prayed for myself and nothing happen. God being the awesome Father that He is didn't scold me or get angry in any way, but He spoke to me and said something that blew my mind. He said that I had to go through this for His Glory and for the good of His people. I didn't understand it, but had a total peace about it as I didn't have to totally understand as I knew that He knew and that was good enough for me. The Lord reminded me that I was to keep declaring that I was already healed because I was, but my going through this and how I handled it would bring Him more Glory and would be good for the people of God.

You must know that God can heal immediately, but doesn't always do so!!!

Examples to consider

(1) There have been countless numbers of people who have encountered family matters that were so traumatic that we needed a miracle to resolve them. That person who has been healthy all his/her life and is living for the Lord as best they know how and goes to the Doctor and gets a devastating diagnosis. Having seen God work miraculously in the lives of others, they're left wondering why He didn't do it for them. I want to encourage you, if that's your testimony as God is still able to heal immediately, but He still has the right not to also. He's not picking on you or mad at you, but rest assured that there is a level of Glory that God is going to get out of how you handle that situation and it's still going to work for your good. Not only will it work for

your good, but those around you will also be blessed by seeing you walk through your tough and trying time still praising and blessing God. So if He doesn't heal right away, know that He can and He has a plan that will somewhere down the line be revealed.

(2) To the person who has been waiting on God regarding a relationship, who has kept yourself pure and resisted the desire to be with someone before marriage. I want to let you know that it's worth the wait and when God brings that person into your life, your life will never be the same. That feeling of loneliness is real and your desire to be loved physically is not wrong, but God will help you to hold out. It's much better to wait for the right one than to suffer the pain of and try to recover from the wrong one. Waiting may seem foolish at times, but it's more foolish to rush into a relationship just for the sake of having a relationship.

(3) There are those who have worked hard and done what was right as far as employment and still can't seem to get ahead. Many have been passed up for promotions and in some cases, even trained those who were

Lessons Learned After Dark

promoted. I want to reassure you that God has not forgotten you. I know that you want Him to move on your behalf right now, but know that whenever He decides to moves, it will be the right time. Your job is to prepare as if the promotion is already yours because it actually is. God's preparing you for greater as you go through the process of waiting, but it's up to you to learn the lessons that will help you to excel at that next level!

Lessons Learned After Dark

<u>In my case</u>

As I mentioned earlier, I was shocked, but not shook when the Lord chose not to heal me on the spot. I had to believe that God's plan was more important than my personal plan. Even though He would have gotten Glory out of the Doctors not being able to find the growth that they initially saw, He wanted Greater Glory! I didn't understand that until I began to go through the process. People that I didn't even know were writing, calling and contacting me on Facebook to say that I was inspiring them by the way that I handled the diagnosis and treatment. They couldn't believe that I was still able to keep office hours, preach every Sunday and teach every Wednesday and still do it all with joy. By going through it without throwing a pity party or asking "why me", I was able to touch some lives that had never even noticed that I existed. God also used my experience to start an unofficial ministry as I'm blessed to be contacted by many who are diagnosed with cancer and who are seeking prayer, advice or some sense of direction as they deal with the initial shock.

The bottom line is God knows what He's doing and we must trust Him to do what's best!

Lessons Learned After Dark

Remember *"our thoughts are not His thoughts, neither our ways His ways"*. Though we are to be growing in Christ-likeness, we will never fully understand why God does what He does, but we must be so confident in Him that even when we're shocked by what comes our way that our faith is not shaken because we know that He knows and that's enough!

Lessons Learned After Dark

Lessons Learned After Dark

Lesson 4

Preaching through a Storm!

Lessons Learned After Dark

Lessons Learned After Dark

Lesson 4
Preaching through a Storm

I know beyond the shadow of a doubt that God called me to preach and for the past 30 years, I've given Him my very best. I've often stated that preaching was like breathing and that if you woke me up at 3 or 4 in the morning, from a deep sleep that I could share a word with you. In this case, that belief would be challenged in a big way as I would be put to the test as I would have days when I didn't physically feel able and yet feel led of God to still stand.

I started my first round of chemotherapy one week after meeting with my Oncologist and his prescribed plan of attack included aggressively attacking the cancer. Of course I made sure to ask about preaching, teaching and keeping office hours at the church and he let me know that if I felt strong enough to do so that I could. He warned me to listen to my body and if I was too tired or weak, rest. So for 7 rounds of chemotherapy, I received my treatment and while sitting with an IV in my arm for 6-7 hours, I listened to praise and worship music and preached to myself. There were times when I felt fairly well while being treated and after treatment, but more often than not, I wasn't feeling it. I'd go home and rest for a while, taking evenings off, except for Wednesdays when I'd get up and go and share with God's people. Saturday became my rest day as I prepared for Sunday and that day off usually energized me enough to stand strong and declare what the Lord had given me.

There were a lot of Sundays where even after resting on Saturday, I woke up feeling like staying in bed. I know that many will say that I should have stayed in bed and let one of the Associate Ministers stand in my stead, but you weren't hearing what I was hearing. The Lord had made clear that my going through this was for His Glory and the good of His people and though I didn't realize exactly what that meant, He made it clear in time. You see my pressing through pain and standing strong even while feeling weak was not me trying to prove a point, but God proving that He is *"my strength in weakness"*. As I began standing and preaching while not physically feeling like doing so, God began to show Himself mighty in ways that I had never experienced. Some of my best preaching was on days when I felt the worse because the Spirit of God had to stand in and through me in ways that were no humanly possible. In my pain, I saw God at a whole different

Lessons Learned After Dark

level and experienced His presence as never before. It was often like an out of body experience as the physically sick and tired Gaylon watched God do an awesome work in and by His Spirit. God got the Glory because people could see that I didn't have the strength to do what God was doing in and through me. God got the Glory and His people were richly blessed and it worked for their good as they too saw God showing Himself mighty. Countless times people stated that they saw God in a different and more glorious way through what He did in and through my experience.

The bottom line is that "I had to endure hardness as a good soldier of Jesus Christ" as backing down or surrendering to the pain was not an option.

Examples to consider

(1) There are those in marriages that are not going as planned. Issues and problems have replaced the joy and laughter that you all once had and you daily wonder if it's really worth it. You feel like you're giving your best, but have questions as to whether the other party is doing the same. It seems like you're living from storm

to storm and heartache to heartache and you really feel like calling it quits. I want to encourage you to understand that pain is often part of the growth process, so hang in there. If you're a brother, ask yourself if you can honestly say that you are *"loving her as Christ loves the church"*? Do you truly show the love of God even when you're upset or disappointed in her behavior or performance? Are you truly giving your total self to the relationship without regards to whether you feel like she is giving her total self? Are you able to say that you are living a sacrificial life in every area of your life? My sister, can you honestly say that you are *"submitting to your own husband"*? Are your expectations for your husband based on what you see in someone else's marriage? Do you compare your marriage to others? Can you truly say that you honor him as the head of your household even when you don't totally agree with him? I'm not talking about endangering yourself by following foolishly, but I'm talking about helping him learn and grow from mistakes that he may make. There is a covenant between each of you and the Lord, are you all keeping the covenant?

Lessons Learned After Dark

(2) There are those who serve in ministry and feel like they're not being used properly by the Pastor that they serve under. You feel like you should be preaching more because you are gifted as well as anointed, but have you considered that if that's true *"your gift will make room for you"*? You must understand that if God placed you under that Pastor, he knows when you're ready for more and will open that door in His own time. There are leaders who want positions and titles because they feel like they are more qualified and have more to offer than the ones around them. What are you basing your qualifications on? Have you proven to be faithful to the ministry in time, talent, and treasure? Has your attitude or work ethic changed since you've been waiting for your promotion? How you serve now will determine where you end up later. *"Be faithful over few things and God will make you ruler of many"*. Get frustrated and slack up and you'll end up losing even that which you now are allowed to oversee. Remember that you're being given the privilege to serve in whatever capacity that you're in! The Pastor that you're serving under is fully responsible for the ministry and

has to do what he/she feels led to do. If you say God led you there, trust Him to do what's best.

Storms will come, but you must remember that they will pass and if you're going to be promoted, you must pass the tests that come along with the storms.

Lessons Learned After Dark

<u>In my case</u>

It was one of the toughest times in my life, but also one of the most rewarding times of my life. Learning to go through truly tough and trying times and doing so without any complaining and without throwing any pity parties helped me to grow. From man's perspective, I had reason to sit down and even feel a little sorry for myself, but from God's perspective, I had to man up and *"be strong in the Lord and the power of His might"*. It was not and could not be about me and my feelings!!!

Lessons Learned After Dark

Lesson 5

What you go through is often not about you!

Lessons Learned After Dark

Lessons Learned After Dark

Lesson 5

What you go through is often not about you!

No matter who you are or how much you love the Lord, life will put you through some changes. When you're going through, it's never fun and in most cases you at least are wondering why you're going through it. I know some deeply spiritual person will say that we should never question why, but I disagree as I believe that every situation in life is an opportunity to learn something of value and I want o know what I'm supposed to learn. To go through something and not learn from it is to waste that God allowed experience and opportunity to grow.

I have to be totally honest, I could see no obvious benefit to going through months of outpatient treatment for cancer, followed by a 3 week hospital stay. The thing that kept me focused was what the Lord told me when I was first diagnosed. He made it clear that I was to go through this "for God's glory and for the good of His people". It kept ringing in my spirit that God was going to be glorified and the people of God would be blessed by my enduring this period in my life. The key was that

Lessons Learned After Dark

I had to go through and could not afford to park and throw a pity party, but had to keep pressing forward.

<u>Examples to consider</u>

(1) There are those who spent their lives taking care of their physical bodies through eating right, exercising, and getting proper amounts of rest only to be diagnosed with some life threatening disease. How confusing it must be to do everything within your power to take care of your body only to find out that you're not immune to sickness and disease. I know of several cases, including myself where people truly tried to take good care of their body and were shocked to find out that devastating diseases don't care about your effort. It may not seem fair, but it's reality and we've got to learn how to go through!!!

(2) There are those who married the love of their life and planned to grow old together only to be struck by a tragedy that changed everything. Whether it's an auto accident, work related incident or some other type of tragedy, it leaves one wondering why it happened and how do they get through it. Whether your loved one life

was taken or they were left in a condition where you become a caregiver rather than a partner in life's journey, you still have questions. The love that you for them gives you the strength and ability to care for them, but inwardly, you still struggle with the happily ever after that has somehow escaped you. As tough as it is, you have to be able to keep pressing forward. To stop and feel sorry for yourself can and often will take over your life and leave you in a state of depression and/or discouragement. Please know that I'm not saying you won't have times where you feel down and discouraged, but you can't afford to stay down. You have to trust God enough to keep getting back up.

Lessons Learned After Dark

<u>In my case</u>

I had walked and jogged 3-4 miles, four to five days a week and though overweight, I worked hard to keep my blood pressure and blood levels at a good level. My check up the year before showed good blood pressure and good blood levels, so I felt pretty good as I continued to try to work on my weight. I actually felt confident that I was getting my health and fitness together and was going to live a long and healthy life, free from any major sicknesses or diseases. The diagnosis woke me up and once I realize that He was not going to heal me instantly, I sought the Lord about what was I to learn from this and why I needed to go through it. I'm glad that the Lord loves me enough to let me ask Him questions without getting angry at me for doing so!!!

Throughout my months of chemotherapy, I went to the clinic, was poked and prodded and spent 5-7 hours with an IV in my vein and still didn't fully understand it. Each week, I went in with a smile on my face, praise songs on my phone's play list, and determined to bless God throughout the process. I never will forget my first treatment when about half way through it, a song spoke to my heart as I listened to it and I lifted my hands with tears flowing and just began to bless God. My wife didn't

Lessons Learned After Dark

know what to do because she wasn't sure if I was praising my way through the pain or just taking a praise break, so she just prayed for me. When I came to myself, she was sitting next to me, wiping tears from my eyes and praying in the spirit. I was reassured that it was all good and whatever I had to go through, I was going to go through it with flying colors.

After completing three and one half months of chemotherapy, I was given a break, so that my body could prepare for the three weeks of inpatient treatment. I kept my regular office hours, taught during our Midweek Celebration and preached on Sundays like all was well. I did so because despite how I felt, in my heart and mind, all was well. The biggest thing to happen was one Sunday after preaching a powerful word and just being soaked from head to toe in sweat, I wiped my face and head and hair started to come out on my towel. You ask why that was so big? Well because I was so confident in God that when my hair didn't come out in chemotherapy, I felt like favor was going to allow me to be able to go through the whole process, with the waves laying smooth. Please know I was not caught up in my hair, but I thought if God wanted to show Himself mighty in that way so be it!

Lessons Learned After Dark

On August 25, 2010 I went through a battery of test to make sure that my body was strong enough for the prescribed treatment. It was a very long day and I was so glad when it was over that I went home and went to bed. Those who know me know that I don't take naps, but I physically was spent. We received a call to verify that all tests were good and I was to go through a series of twice a day shots for a week in preparation for stem cells to be collected. The shots worked and they were able to collect the needed stem cells for the transplant. They set my admission date for September 21, 2010 and now we just had to rest and wait.

September 21, 2010 finally arrived and I was admitted to the special unit for those who were having or recovering from stem cell transplants. From day one they began to take blood several times a day, with the last one being around 3:30 every morning. I didn't get much sleep because they not only had to check my blood levels, but they also check my pressure around the clock. I had the transplant on day 7 and from then on felt a little weak, but I was determined to go through in a way that gave God glory. Even when I was tired or in pain, I kept smiling and being kind to all whom I came in contact with. I took my own pajamas and clothes that were heavy starched and

Lessons Learned After Dark

every morning I got up, put on my clothes and took a walk around the hospital. I greeted everyone with the joy of Jesus and stopped by the prayer garden to spend some special time with the Lord. The Lord was so gracious that I only lost my appetite for 3 days and only had one real episode of sickness where I couldn't hold anything on my stomach for about 2 hours. Each day following that episode I seemed to be getting a little stronger and feeling a little better.

Each day, I post an update on Facebook to let my family and friends know that God was showing Himself mighty each day. I was surprised by the response as I heard from many people that I didn't know personally who stated that my post helped them through things that they were going through. It was then that I began to see what the Lord meant when He said it was "to His glory and for the good of His people". I continued to progress and on October 12, 2010, I was dismissed 4 days earlier than expected. My recovery required that I be homebound for 2 additional weeks, with little or no contact except for my family. I was able to share in the worship through Skype, but couldn't wait until they released me to return to worship and life as I'd known it.

Lessons Learned After Dark

My wife and I counted down the days and everyday she and my daughter watched me closely to see if I seemed to be getting stronger. I continued to get stronger and feel better and was excited about the return to corporate worship. I wouldn't tell my wife, but I was still feeling like I had a long way to go to be myself again and though excited, I still had to pray away some apprehension.

Lessons Learned After Dark

Lessons Learned After Dark

Conclusion of the Matter

Lessons Learned After Dark

Lessons Learned After Dark

Conclusion of the Matter

On the final Sunday in October 2010, I returned to church and the pulpit where I'm blessed to serve and it was a triumphant return. Though I didn't physically feel 100%, I was as excited as a child at Christmas. Me and the family had our preparation period and 10:30 finally came and we left for Morning Celebration (they didn't want me to get there before 10:45). We arrived and they had cleared the foyer prior to leading us there, so that we could go in and join the Celebration.

The doors opened and my heart leaped with joy as I saw a House filled with the people that I'm blessed to Pastor on their feet cheering and blessing God. We walked about half way down the middle aisle and I guess I must have been moving too slow as my wife became a sprinter and ran to the altar and exploded into worship. We worshipped and cried and worshipped and cried for the first 15 minutes or so of the celebration. When I came to myself, all I could say was "it's good to be here" as for that moment in time, I could actually feel what Peter meant on the Mount of Transfiguration. The Glory of God was so think that you could almost hold it in your hand!

Lessons Learned After Dark

The choir sang like never before and the flow of the Celebration was at a level as never before. When I stood to give my text, I again had to gather myself and though physically a little tired and emotionally overwhelmed, the Spirit of God empowered me to preach with power and authority. My message was "It Had to Happen" and by sharing the text and my personal testimony, God used me mightily. He had me to remind the Saints that life doesn't always seem fair and at times we won't understand why we're going through what we have to go through, but if He allows it, it has to happen and it'll work for our good.

The truth of the matter is that some lessons we can't learn until we're in a dark place in our lives. It's during those times when we can see the Lord more clearly and better understand what He's been trying to teach us. There are lessons to learn everyday, but it's up to you to become a learner of the lessons. You can learn them and get better or refuse to learn and become bitter!!!

I must admit that there have been additional challenges since my return to the pulpit. Some more painful than others, but even the most painful ones have taught me some valuable lessons. I've truly learned how to trust in God with my whole heart and to be confident that He will come through on my behalf.

I thank God for Lessons Learned After Dark!!!

Lessons Learned After Dark

Lessons Learned After Dark

Pastor Foreman is available for inspirational speaking engagements, book signings and survivor testimonial events.

Contact Information

Gaylon Foreman

1020 E. Herring Ave

Waco, Texas 76704

gp4man@aol.com

www.carverpark.org

(254) 799-2766

FACEBOOK

Lessons Learned After Dark

Made in the USA
Charleston, SC
07 February 2013